actionable
evaluation
basics

actionable
evaluation
basics

Getting succinct answers to the most important questions

E. Jane Davidson, Ph.D.

Real Evaluation

Actionable evaluation for the real world

Print Edition (December, 2013)

Also available as an e-book:

in English

in Spanish (*Principios Básicos de la Evaluación para la Acción: Obteniendo respuestas sucintas a las preguntas más importantes [minilibro]* – translated by Pablo Rodriguez-Bilella)

and soon to be published in French (*Les essentiels de l'évaluation tournée vers l'action : Obtenir des réponses succinctes aux questions les plus importantes* – translated by Ghislain Arbour)

For information, please contact the publisher:

Real Evaluation Ltd.
Auckland, New Zealand
Email: jane@RealEvaluation.com
http://RealEvaluation.com

Contents

Evaluation isn't that hard, is it?.................................1

What is Actionable Evaluation?...............................3

What goes wrong when evaluation is unactionable?............5

The Six Key Elements of Actionable Evaluation 7

1. clear purpose 9

2. the right stakeholder engagement strategy...............11

3. important, big-picture questions 14

4. well-reasoned answers...................................20

5. succinct, straight-to-the-point reporting..............40

6. actionable insights 45

Conclusions...49

Resources & more information 53

About the author 55

Evaluation isn't that hard, is it?

Do you ever get frustrated with people who think that all there is to evaluation is picking a few indicators and measuring them? The same ones who think all qualitative and even mixed method work is fluffy and unreliable?

And, on the other hand, have you ever read (or written!) an evaluation report and still wondered yourself how worthwhile the outcomes really were or whether the entire program (or project, policy, etc.) was in fact a complete waste of time, effort, and money?

At one level, we can understand managers' needing direct answers to their important questions – and trackable progress they can visualize.

But how can evaluators deliver on that without massively oversimplifying the richness we see in project, program, and policy design, implementation, and outcomes?

Introducing actionable evaluation!

What is the essence of actionable evaluation? What are its key ingredients? How do you go about doing – or commissioning – actionable evaluation?

In a nutshell, there are <u>six elements</u> that are essential to actionable evaluation:

1. a clear purpose for the evaluation;

2. the right stakeholder engagement strategy;

3. important, big-picture questions to guide the whole evaluation;

4. well-reasoned answers to the big-picture questions, backed by a convincing mix of evidence;

5. succinct, straight to the point reporting that doesn't get lost in the details; and

6. answers and insights that are actionable, that we can do something with.

This short minibook provides a quick overview of these six elements, and the other important concepts and methodologies covered in Dr. Jane Davidson's popular workshops on Actionable Evaluation.

~~~~~~~~~~~

What is Actionable Evaluation?

Actionable evaluation is real, genuine, practical evaluation that people can actually use. It is well-evidenced, but doesn't get lost in the details or become obsessed with indicators, metrics, or methods. Actionable evaluation is based on sound, evidence-informed, evaluative reasoning. It asks the most important questions about quality, value, and importance – and delivers straight-to-the-point, actionable answers.

Actionable evaluation:

a) is clearly relevant to the key actions, decisions, and thinking of those the evaluation needs to inform;

b) goes right to the heart of what is really important, and doesn't get lost in the details;

c) favors approximate answers to important questions over accuracy to four decimal places on trivia;

d) resists being lured into a focus on the outcomes that are most easily measured;

e) presents findings in a way that is simple, but not simplistic;

f) is useful — at both strategic and practical (or operational) levels;

g) influences and clarifies thinking, action, and decision-making; and

h) gives insights that help people figure out what actions to take.

n evaluation it is incredibly easy to get lost in methods and measurement.

If you are guided by an actionable evaluation framework, you will be clear that evaluation is not only about measures and analysis methods; evaluation is about delivering clear, well-reasoned answers to the most important questions.

Actionable evaluation reporting is succinct and straight-to-the-point, but gets its arms around the whole story, not just a narrow and misleading slice of it.

~~~~~~~~~~

What goes wrong when evaluation is unactionable?

We have all seen examples of evaluations that, although they appeared on the surface to be technically adequate, somehow totally missed the mark.

I recall a few years ago being asked to review a set of evaluations of similar programs for a government agency. They generally appeared to be plausible pieces of work, particularly to the untrained eye. There didn't seem to be anything technically 'wrong' with them, but somehow they weren't useful for informing thinking or action.

As I looked through the reports, several themes became obvious to me. And on discussing with another colleague who had been asked to complete a similar task for another agency, we found that these were not isolated issues.

Evaluation that is unactionable:

- tends to leap to measurement or data gathering without a clear sense of who or what the evaluation is for – i.e., its purpose

- often fails to involve the right people, or involve them at the wrong time or in the wrong way

- asks questions that are too narrow and detailed (e.g., at the indicator level); it fails to ask the most important things, or there may be no questions at all

- forgets the "so what" – it presents summaries of quantitative and/or qualitative evidence as though it *is* the answer; it's not!

- gets totally lost in the details; the reader has to struggle through data, searching and searching for the answer to the question

- produces findings and conclusions that leave you still unclear where and why to take action.

~~~~~~~~~~

The Six Key Elements
of Actionable Evaluation

What are the key ingredients we need to make sure we get real, genuine, actionable evaluation?

In my experience, we need the following six elements:

1) a clear purpose for the evaluation;

2) the right stakeholder engagement strategy;

3) important, big-picture evaluation questions to guide the whole evaluation;

4) *actual answers* to the big-picture questions, backed by transparent reasoning and a convincing mix of evidence;

5) succinct, straight to the point reporting that doesn't get lost in the details; and

6) answers and insights that are actionable, that we can do something with.

Let's explore each of these in more detail.

~~~~~~~~~~~

1. clear purpose

All good evaluation starts with a utilization focus. We need to ask *who* needs to learn *what*, for what *purpose*, by *when*, and to what *level of certainty*.

Note that we should *not* be leaping to measurement here, as so often happens. We need to focus on the broad decisions or actions, and how evaluation needs to inform them.

What kinds of actions or decisions might evaluation support? Usually it is at least two or three of the following:

- Informing citizens, taxpayers, funders, or shareholders about how wisely their money and other resources are being invested to achieve what most needs to be achieved

- Informing consumer choice about which products, services, programs, or organizations they should buy, enroll in, work for, etc.

- Informing strategic decisions about which policies, programs, products, or services to expand, scale down, invest in further, or discontinue

- Informing improvements in programs, policies, services, etc., and their implementation

- Informing the design, conceptualization, or development of new strategies, policies, programs, projects, or approaches

- Building capability within the organization and/or the community for outcomes-focused strategy, program design, monitoring, adaptive management, and/or evaluation.

~~~~~~~~~~

2. the right stakeholder engagement strategy

The next major decision is <u>who</u> needs to be involved, <u>what</u> is the best way of engaging with them, and <u>where</u> in the evaluation process?

There are opportunities to engage people in logic modeling, the formulation of evaluation questions, the process of defining quality and value, evidence gathering, sense making, reporting, and action planning.

Whose voices should be at the table for each of these tasks?

Getting the stakeholder engagement strategy right has implications for evaluation validity, justice, credibility, utilization, and cost.

Validity. Whose expertise do we need in order to get this right? Drawing on the right mix of stakeholder expertise helps us ensure evaluation validity.

Justice. Who has a *right* to be part of the conversation at each point in the evaluation? There are important justice considerations here for including the voices that have historically been excluded, particularly those from the community, actual and potential program recipients, and program beneficiaries/impactees.

Credibility. Whose involvement is needed to give the evaluation credibility, particularly in the eyes of funders, political supporters, potential critics, naysayers, and opponents? The "who" and the "how" of stakeholder involvement are just as important as the "what" for the credibility of the evaluation and its findings.

Utilization. Whose buy-in and commitment do we most need to maximize the chances of the evaluation being used? Stakeholder involvement influences utilization, not just of findings, but of the knowledge, know-how, and capabilities that evaluation can help build.

Cost. And finally, stakeholder involvement comes with time and monetary costs which must be taken into consideration. Although sometimes costly, it is often true that time invested now and getting people to deeply understand what's working well or not can generate powerful buy-in and ownership of the change going forward.

Involvement ≠ validity

A common trap in collaborative evaluation is to assume that if the evaluation somehow involves all the various stakeholder groups, this basically guarantees validity because all relevant voices have been heard.

Unfortunately, evaluation is not that simple. It's not just about *who* was at the table; it's also about *whether they got the evaluation right*.

Truly worthwhile engagement in evaluation expertly guides people through a well-designed process, supported by tools and frameworks, that allows them to ask the right questions, answer them validly, present the findings credibly and compellingly, and formulate well-grounded action plans.

Good collaborative evaluation is not just a facilitation role; it is a serious business, and a lot more challenging than it looks.

Externality/independence ≠ validity

There's also a flipside to the first trap. Just because your evaluator is independent and external doesn't mean you automatically have validity either!

Nor does a long list of impressive credentials, or the 'brand recognition' of a big consulting firm.

Again, it's not just about *who* did the evaluation; it's also about *whether they got it right*.

Importantly, there is a pervasive assumption in many cultures that independence and externality are essential for credibility. But there are cases where independence and a lack of connectedness can actually damage credibility *and* validity. For an explanation of this, see my post on Genuine Evaluation: *Credibility and independence in evaluation - an alternative view.*[1]

---

[1] http://genuineevaluation.com/credibility-and-independence-in-evaluation-an-alternative-view/

3. important, big-picture questions

Many evaluations get lost in the details. One of the main causes is having no clear sense of "What are we trying to find out here?"

A useful way to improve relevance is to have a short list of 'big-picture' questions guiding the entire evaluation. Too often, evaluations don't have any of these big-picture questions; they just leap to measurement or data gathering. Or, they ask incredibly narrow questions, at the indicator level.

This happens because people are thinking, "What can I measure?" rather than "What do we really need to know?"

John Tukey, a famous statistician, once said: "Far better an approximate answer to the right question, which is often vague, than an exact answer to the wrong question, which can always be made precise."

Truly relevant evaluation hinges on having the right questions to guide the work. The right questions may be hard to answer; you may only be able to get approximate answers; but it is still important to ask the questions that really matter.

Explicitly evaluative questions

In evaluation, the right questions to guide the entire evaluation are *explicitly evaluative* questions. Let me show you what I mean by that, using some examples.

When asking about implementation, a *monitoring* question might ask, "Was the program implemented as intended?" or "Was it implemented according to specifications?" In contrast, an *evaluative* question would ask *how well* it was implemented — was it implemented thoroughly, fairly, ethically, culturally appropriately, efficiently, professionally, in a way consistent with relevant legal and professional standards, etc.?

When looking at program reach or coverage, a monitoring question would ask *how many* people were reached and/or *how* were they reached. An evaluative question would ask, "*How adequate* was program reach?"

In other words, we would ask not just how many people, but did we reach *enough* people? Did we reach the *right* people?

We would ask not just how it was done, but *how well* it was done. Did we use the best avenues and methods we could have? How well did we access hard-to-reach populations? Did we reach those with the greatest need? Who missed out, and was that fair, ethical, just?

When asking questions about outcomes, it's not just what changed or whether targets and goals were met; the question is: *"How substantial and valuable* were the outcomes?"

How well did they meet the most important needs and help realize the most important aspirations? Should they be considered truly impressive, mediocre, or unacceptably weak? Were they not just statistically significant, but educationally, socially, economically, and practically significant? Did they make a real difference in people's lives? Were the outcomes worth achieving given the effort and investment put into obtaining them?

What should be included in this short list of big-picture evaluation questions?

A special treat for my readers – my "cheat sheet" of big-picture evaluation questions! Simply reword to fit whatever you are evaluating. And, of course, each question may be broken out into further subquestions.

1. *Was the program – and is still – needed? How well does it address the most important root causes? Is it still the right solution?*

   For any evaluation, you will always need a question about the <u>need for the initiative</u> and whether it addresses the true causes of the problem.

Note here another *key difference between monitoring and evaluation*. The need for the program is generally assumed in monitoring, which basically asks whether a program is on time, on target, and on budget. In evaluation, it is part of our job to ask this question about the need for the program. After all an on-target program that is no longer needed isn't a good or worthwhile one. And evaluation, by definition, would say so.

2. *How well designed and implemented is the program?*

Most evaluations also require a <u>process evaluation</u> question. This high-level question would be unpacked to ask about the quality of content, design, and delivery/implementation of the program. This includes the key outputs such as the products and services delivers, coverage and reach, and so forth. Again, note that we are not just asking *what* the outputs (etc.) are; we are asking *how good* they are.

3. *How valuable are the outcomes for [insert impactee group]?*

Virtually all evaluations will need an <u>outcome evaluation</u> question. This asks how substantially something has changed for people. It also asks whether the change is large enough and fast enough to address the identified needs, aspirations, and opportunities.

You may break this question out into subquestions that ask about different impactee groups, different contexts, and different outcomes.

4. What works best for whom, under what conditions, and why/how?

If you are planning to use the evaluation for program conceptualization, design, or development, you will need to know not just whether the program works, but <u>under what conditions, for whom, and why</u> the program works best. You will also need to know this for significant streamlining or redesign.

This is what realist evaluators[2] refer to as 'context', which incidentally does not simply mean location. 'Context' is the set of conditions required in order to 'fire' the causal mechanism(s) by which the program achieves its effects. Information about the context and causal mechanisms is also important if the client is trying to decide where and to which communities and recipients to expand a particular program.

Getting a sound understanding of causal mechanisms can be informed greatly by logic modeling – see Funnell & Rogers' (2011) *Purposeful Program Theory*.[3] This comprehensive and thoughtful guide even explores how best to do this for simple, complicated, and complex aspects of programs and other evaluands.

5. How worthwhile was it overall? Or, Which parts or aspects of the program generated the most valuable outcomes for the time, money, and effort we invested?

---

[2] [For a good introduction to realist evaluation, check out Dr. Gill Westhorpe's site at Community Matters: http://www.communitymatters.com.au/gpage1.html

[3] Available in hard copy or ebook from http://www.amazon.com/dp/0470478578

If you're making strategic decisions about further investing in this project vs. others in your strategic portfolio, you will need some sense of whether the outcomes were worth the time, effort, and other resources put in.

6. How sustainable is the impact? How sustainable is the program itself?

If long-term <u>sustainability</u> of positive change is a priority, you will need a question that asks whether the impacts are sustained or whether they 'slip back' after a period of time.

You might also ask: How sustainable is the program itself? Could it survive a change in leadership or a reduction in funding now that it is no longer in the set-up phase?

Those of you familiar with Michael Scriven's Key Evaluation Checklist[4] will recognize that questions 2 and 3 would fall under the SubEvaluations checkpoints in the KEC, while question 5 is similar to Scriven's Overall Significance checkpoint.

A major point of departure between my list above and the KEC is the importance I place on understanding something of the *why and how*, through smart use of program theory and realist evaluation.

I'm not saying these are always needed – I do many evaluations that don't use them – but for certain evaluations they are very valuable if done right, and certainly shouldn't be skipped over without due consideration.

---

[4] The latest version of the KEC is available on Michael Scriven's website http://michaelscriven.info

4. well-reasoned answers

You would think that once we get the right questions in place, the answers would be automatically forthcoming. Unfortunately not!

Here's how I've seen even some very good evaluation questions answered. These may be familiar to you ...

The "Rorschach inkblot" approach

There is an assessment tool called the Rorschach inkblot test[5] used by psychiatrists to psychoanalyze patients by asking them to describe what they see in an abstract-looking ink blot. Of course, everyone sees something different.

---

[5] http://en.wikipedia.org/wiki/Rorschach_test

When evaluation reports are vague and don't give clear answers, they resemble a Rorschach inkblot in that people can read what they like into the findings.

When this happens, the evaluation team is actually opting out of its job – which is *actually answering* the evaluative questions.

Implicitly they are saying to the client, "You work it out."

The "divine judgment" approach

Sometimes we do see direct answers to evaluative questions, but the reasoning is kept well hidden. It is as if the evaluator is saying to us. "I looked upon it and saw that it was good" (as God supposedly did on the 7th day).

These are the kinds of reports with sweeping conclusions and recommendations that seem to come out of nowhere. The evaluation can seem to be very subjective or opinion-based.

And the client might wonder, *Who does the evaluator think they are?*

[Only supernatural beings have no need to justify their reasoning.]

Evaluative reasoning

What does it take to deliver well-reasoned and well-evidenced direct answers in a way that is systematic and transparent? Consider this recent comment from Michael Quinn Patton regarding Michael Scriven's contribution to conceptualizing what evaluation is really all about.

Michael Scriven

Patton says:

> "Moreover, and this is critically important, [Scriven] shows that valuing is fundamentally about reasoning and critical thinking. Evaluation as a field has become methodologically manic obsessive. Too many of us, and those who commission us, think it's all about methods. It's not. It's all about reasoning."
>
> – New Directions for Evaluation[6], vol. 133, p. 105

---

[6] http://onlinelibrary.wiley.com/doi/10.1002/ev.v2012.133/issuetoc

Evaluative reasoning is the piece that makes evaluation fundamentally different from descriptive research.

Evaluations should generate not just evidence, but <u>evaluative conclusions</u>.

Evaluative conclusions tell us not just "what's so" (e.g., what the outcomes are); they also tell us "so what" (how *good, valuable, or worthwhile* the outcomes are).

"So what" is a difficult question to answer, but fundamentally important for evaluation to genuinely inform decision-making.

Using a diagram, we might also explain evaluative reasoning like this.

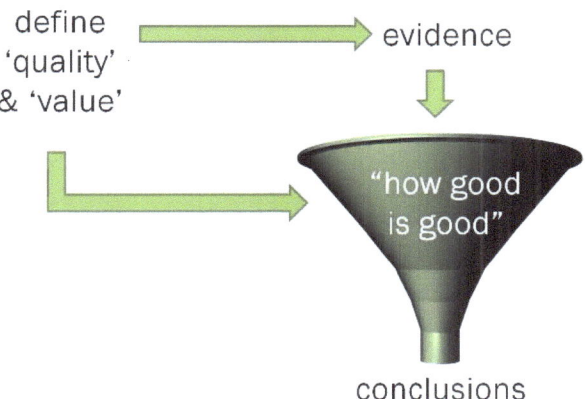

To begin, we need to define what is meant by "quality" and "value" for a particular program, policy, initiative, or whatever we are evaluating. Obviously, a lot of groundwork goes into this, such as strengths and needs assessment.[7]

---

[7] For more detail on defining criteria, see my book, Evaluation Methodology Basics: The nuts and bolts of sound evaluation (Sage, 2005). http://realevaluation.com/read/book/

This process generates two things: (1) the criteria of merit, which are the *aspects* of design, implementation, and outcomes, and cost-effectiveness we look at to determine whether performance is any good or not; and (2) the definitions of "how good is good" (the "evaluative interpretation funnel").

From the criteria of merit, we work out what mix of evidence we should gather and examine.

When we build the "evaluative interpretation funnel", we define what mix of evidence would convince us we have *high quality* program design, *excellent* implementation, *highly valuable* outcomes, and *excellent value* from the overall investment.

Once we gather the evidence, we pass it through our "evaluative interpretation funnel", work through the interpretation and sensemaking process, and that is where we draw our evaluative conclusions.

The upfront process of thinking through what 'excellent' would look like — as opposed to 'good', 'just acceptable', or 'unacceptable' — is crucial for getting to evaluative conclusions.

The criteria tell us what evidence we will need to gather. And our definition of "how good is good" tells us how to interpret that evidence.

What tools or frameworks can we use for the all-important task of defining how good is good?

One extremely useful tool is the evaluative rubric.

Evaluative rubrics paint a picture of what the evidence should look like at different levels of performance.

Evaluative rubrics example 1

Let me give an example from the system used in New Zealand for quality assurance in higher education. Institutes of Technology and Polytechnics (ITPs) and most other higher education and training organizations conduct a self-review in which they are required to answer six key evaluation questions[8]:

1. How well do learners achieve?

2. What is the value of the outcomes for key stakeholders, including learners?

3. How well do programs and activities match the needs of learners and other stakeholders?

4. How effective is the teaching?

5. How well are learners guided and supported?

6. How effective are governance and management in supporting educational achievement?

Each key evaluation question must be answered relative to a generic rubric like the following[9]:

---

[8]	http://www.nzqa.govt.nz/providers-partners/self-assessment/make-self-assessment-happen/tools-and-resources/key-evaluation-questions/

[9] Rubric reproduced here with permission of NZQA. To access all rubrics used under this system, see **NZQA's full set of rubrics** at http://www.nzqa.govt.nz/assets/Providers-and-partners/Registration-and-accreditation/External-evaluation/eer-rubrics-revised.pdf

Excellent

- Performance is clearly exemplary in relation to the question.

- Very few or no gaps or weaknesses.

- Any gaps or weaknesses have no significant impact and are managed effectively.

Good

- Performance is generally strong in relation to the question.

- Few gaps or weaknesses.

- Gaps or weaknesses have some impact but are mostly managed effectively.

Adequate

- Performance is inconsistent in relation to the question.

- Some gaps or weaknesses have impact, and are not managed effectively.

- Meets minimum expectations/requirements as far as can be determined.

Poor

- Performance is unacceptably weak in relation to the question.

- Significant gaps or weaknesses are not managed effectively.

- Does not meet minimum expectations/requirements

The evaluative interpretation step

Suppose you determine that performance was "good" on one of the questions. How do you justify that conclusion in a clear, transparent, and explicitly evaluative way under this framework?

Let's look at the pieces in the definition (the three bullet points):

- Performance is <u>generally strong</u> in relation to the question.

- Few gaps or weaknesses.

- Gaps or weaknesses have some impact but are mostly managed effectively.

Rubrics demand systematic use of evaluative inference to draw conclusions.

For example, when rating "good", you would need to show, specifically, what evidence led you to believe performance was "generally strong," – as opposed to "clearly exemplary" (excellent) or "inconsistent" (adequate).

Second, what were the gaps or weaknesses, and why should they be considered "few" in number?

Third, what impact did the gaps and weaknesses have? Finally what exactly is the organization doing to manage gaps and weaknesses, and why do you consider this "effective management"?

Evaluative rubrics example 2

Rubrics may be used to guide evaluative conversations, particularly when it's important to help stakeholders see for themselves how they are doing and where the most important opportunities for improvement lie.

Rubrics may be used to capture baseline or diagnostic evidence, as well as for tracking outcomes.

This next example encompasses all of these applications.

The following framework is from an example of an intervention designed to accelerate the achievement of indigenous and minority students and students with special education needs in schools.[10]

Acceleration of student achievement is achieved through having practitioners coach and guide a school change team (consisting of school leaders, teachers, parents[11], and local tribal or community representatives) in root cause diagnosis, change management, and evaluation of what works.

---

[10] This framework and the associated rubrics are owned by the New Zealand Ministry of Education, and are used to support its Student Achievement Function initiative. Excerpts are reproduced here with the Ministry's permission. For further details, please access the following links:

http://www.minedu.govt.nz/theMinistry/EducationInitiatives/StrengtheningStudentAc hievement/StudentAchievementFunction.aspx

http://www.edgazette.govt.nz/Articles/Article.aspx?ArticleId=8560

[11] The term *whānau* in the diagram on the next page is similar to the Hawaiian term `*ohana* and refers to extended family, to reflect the wider involvement of grandparents, uncles, aunts, and others in raising and educating children.

Schools learn how to diagnose for themselves where in five key areas they most need to increase their school capability (see diagram); select the right mix of interventions; and then drive through and monitor the change all the way to student achievement outcomes.

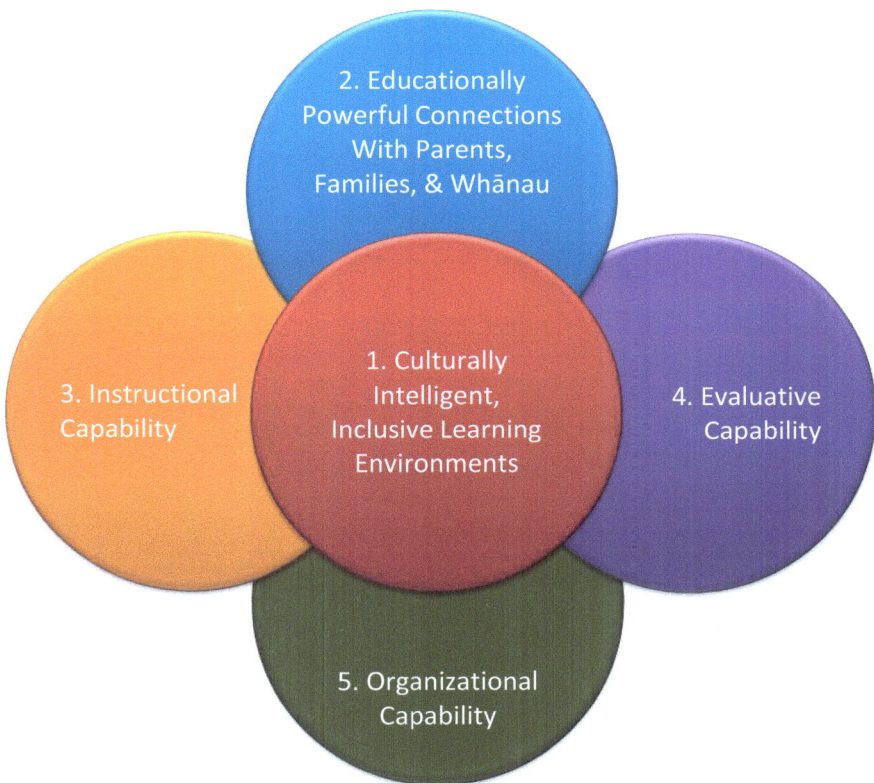

Each of the capabilities has a specific evaluation question and definition of what is covered. For example:

1. Culturally intelligent, inclusive learning environments

Evaluation question: *How well have you created a sense of belonging for all learners to help them connect with what they learn, how they learn, and who they learn with?*

Aspects covered:

a) Bringing to life learners' identities, languages, and cultures in teaching and learning

b) Being proactive about adapting learning environments and/or teaching approaches to allow better access to the curriculum for the learners who need it most;

c) Maintaining a responsive and inclusive organizational culture where there is a pervasive belief that all learners can and will achieve; and

d) Ensuring educators can connect with and engage Māori (indigenous) learners, Pasifika learners, & learners with special education needs and use teaching as inquiry to modify approaches.

Unlike the previous (NZQA) example with a generic rubric, here, *each* capability has a quite detailed rubric describing what the evidence would look like at five different levels of capability:

- high capability

- consolidating capability

- developing capability

- basic capability

- low capability

For example, taking just one of the four elements of culturally intelligent, inclusive learning environments:

1c. Maintaining a responsive and inclusive organizational culture where there is a pervasive belief that all learners can and will achieve

High capability: Leaders (including Boards of Trustees, a group of parents elected by parents to govern the school) clearly make it a strategic priority to proactively create and sustain culturally intelligent, inclusive environments, particularly for Māori learners, Pasifika learners and learners with special education needs, including those learners transitioning from schooling where the language and/or methods of instruction were different. They are highly skilled at leading and changing this aspect of organizational culture for the benefit of learners. Their genuine personal commitment to inclusiveness is evidenced in their clear and deep knowledge of who their learners are, what they pay attention to, how swiftly they identify and react to emerging issues, how they advocate for minority groups, how adequately they resource and do the most important things, build their own knowledge, etc.

Consolidating capability: Leaders (including Boards of Trustees) clearly make it a priority to create and sustain culturally intelligent, inclusive environments, particularly for Māori learners, Pasifika learners and learners with special education needs, including those learners transitioning from schooling where the language and/or methods of instruction were different. They are skilled at leading and changing this aspect of organizational culture for the benefit of learners. Leaders' genuine personal commitment to inclusiveness is evidenced in how they use a good knowledge of who their learners are, advocate for minority groups, how adequately they resource and do the most important things, build their own knowledge, etc. However, not all issues are picked up and addressed quickly, or using sufficiently creative approaches to resourcing.

Developing capability: Leaders (including Boards of Trustees) are actively working to create and sustain culturally intelligent, inclusive environments, particularly for Māori learners, Pasifika learners and learners with special education needs, including those learners transitioning from schooling where the language and/or methods of instruction were different. They monitor the school or kura [indigenous Māori language immersion school] culture, identify and react to emerging issues, but may not always address the most crucial issues first and fast. There may also be some misalignment between resourcing decisions and priorities. Leaders generally support minority groups and are starting to build their own knowledge of the identities, languages and cultures of their learners. They are developing skills in leading and changing organizational culture.

Basic capability: Leaders acknowledge the need to create and sustain culturally intelligent, inclusive environments, but may still struggle to visualize what this looks like for Māori learners, Pasifika learners and learners with special education needs. They are likely to have a need to develop skills in leading and changing organizational culture. Responses to emerging issues are well intentioned but may be reactive, tardy, or show significant misalignment between resourcing decisions and priorities. Negative stereotyping of particular groups of learners (by ethnicity, family connection, etc.) is not generally tolerated, but could be challenged more effectively.

Low capability: Leader talk is "I treat everyone the same"; the need for culturally intelligent, inclusive environments is not genuinely accepted. Negative stereotyping of particular groups of learners (by ethnicity, family connection, etc.) may go unchallenged. Issues relating to school or kura culturally intelligent responsiveness and inclusiveness tend to remain undetected or unaddressed for significant lengths of time, to the detriment of learners. Leaders are likely to require significant support and oversight to develop an awareness of how they can and do influence organizational culture through their actions and inaction.

Generic vs. specific rubrics

Evaluative rubrics may be written as generic (one or more broad rubrics to cover multiple evaluation questions or criteria) or specific (one rubric for each key criterion, written specifically with that criterion in mind).

The Student Achievement Function rubrics are very much at the detailed/specific end of the scale, whereas the NZQA rubrics are at the broad/generic end.

Whether rubrics are generic or specific, or something in between, the most important part of the evaluation process is the collective sense making of the evidence using the rubric. As many who have used these tools agree, the ratings generated are often far less important than the rich, evaluative conversations that happen on the journey to drawing the conclusions.

Simple but not simplistic

Another of the truly useful things about rubrics is this: Although there is incredibly rich detail behind each one, it is possible to summarize to give a simple and easily understandable visual representation of progress.

For the Student Achievement Function, for example, you could show the baseline data at the beginning, progress at the end of the intervention, and then also the additional progress made after the intervention has ended.

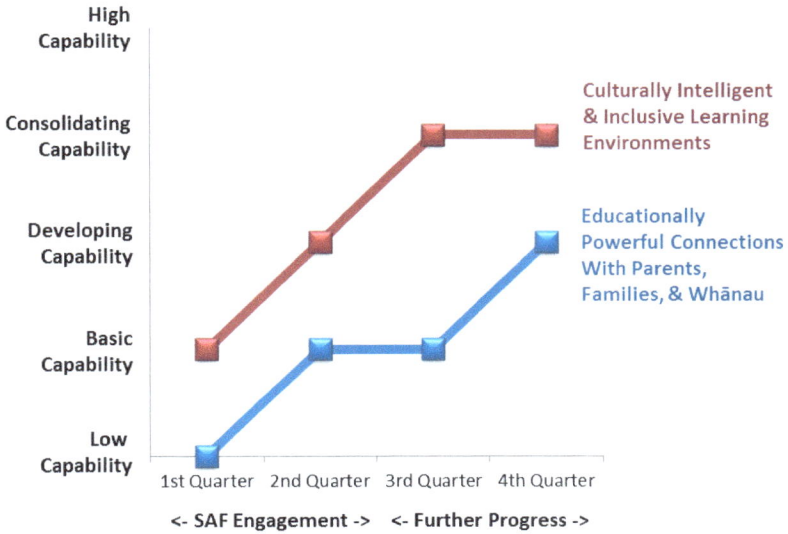

This is very different from simply graphing a single indicator because each of these points represents such a rich body of evidence that captures virtually all (or, at least, much closer to all) of what the capability means.

In other words, by using rubrics to rate outcomes, we can get a representation of progress that is simple but not simplistic.

Why rubrics? Why not just indicators?

Most outcomes we might be interested in cover a fairly broad domain. In psychology we would have called this the 'construct'.

We define this outcome domain (construct) with a list of concepts that cover the 'space' — much like the list of what is covered under each of the capabilities in the Student Achievement Function framework.

The term "indicators" is usually used to refer to very specific, quantitative measures that *sample* across that domain (see below).

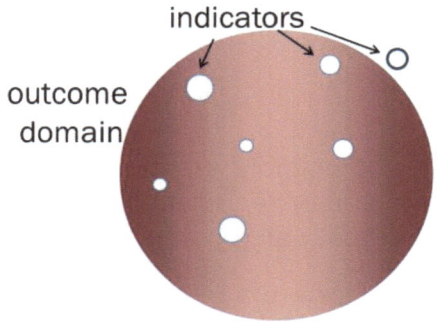

Each indicator covers only a very small space, and some are not really even part of the domain (i.e. part of the very definition of what quality or value is for that domain), but they are correlated with it. Indicators are generally easy to measure, precise, narrow, and — most importantly — manipulable.[12]

---

[12] For more on this topic, see the entry under Indicators in Michael Scriven's entertaining and brilliant *Evaluation Thesaurus* (1991, Sage Publications): http://www.sagepub.com/books/Book3562

This means that it is sometimes possible for a program to look good on the indicators, but not actually be of very high value. And conversely, a program that actually does have high value and quality might look weak based on its indicators because they do not cover what is most important about performance.

Of course, we are all familiar with this notion in performance appraisal, one branch of personnel evaluation! Have you ever felt that your performance appraisal didn't fairly or accurately capture the value you'd been adding in your work? Exactly …

In contrast, "true criteria" (in the sense I refer to them here) are broader and messier definitions of performance on that outcome domain.

Criteria are harder to measure, approximate, broad-brush, but relatively unmanipulable. What this means is, if the rubric is very well designed, and if program staff try to manipulate the performance of the program so that it looks good on the rubrics, then the program really *will* be performing well.

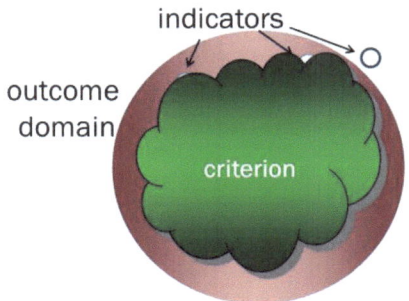

With rubrics, we are seeking to create something that is more like one of these broad 'criteria' that covers virtually all of what is most important about the outcome domain. We are looking for an approximate answer that "gets its arms around" the *whole* of the important question rather than precision on narrow points of interest (the indicators).

Where and how indicators *should* be used

It is important to note that indicators *can and should* be used in most evaluation. But their place is not as "the answers"; they are part of the mix of evidence that is considered in formulating well-reasoned answers to evaluative questions.

Even when you capture process or outcome evidence using indicators, you still need to do the evaluative interpretation step. This is best done through a process that considers the other evidence (quantitative and/or qualitative) pertaining to that domain of performance.

For that reason, we often see indicators or metrics included *within* evaluative rubrics *alongside* other evidence.

So, I am <u>not</u> suggesting that we throw out all indicators in favor of rubrics.

I am suggesting that we should (1) consider indicators alongside other evidence when we look at performance on a particular aspect of quality or performance and (2) be systematic and transparent about how we define "how good is good" for that mix of evidence (including any indicators).

A brief note about the origins of rubrics (for me)

As an aside, I first started developing and using performance rubrics – *but for performance appraisal* – as part of my work in a human resources role in 1995-1996. This was prior to heading for the United States and 'discovering' evaluation in the course of my doctoral studies. The methodology seemed to fit well with the logic of evaluation, particularly the merit determination step, and I have been using it for that purpose ever since.

Of course, rubrics have for many years been used in education for grading essays and other forms of student assessment that required expert judgment rather than mechanistic scoring. So, it's not surprising to see rubrics being used more and more in the evaluation of programs and policies.

For more detail on evaluative rubrics, please see my *Evaluation Methodology Basics* textbook (2005, Sage), and sign up to my free mailing list to hear about webinars and other opportunities to learn more of the theory and the 'how to': http://realevaluation.com/about/join/register-2/

~~~~~~~~~~

5. succinct, straight-to-the-point reporting

Reporting can make or break the relevance of evaluation for different audiences. In this section, I discuss some common problems with reporting, the key characteristics of great reporting, and some concrete suggestions for how to get this every time.

Characteristics of poor evaluation reporting

Some of the great problems with evaluation reports include:

- being excessively long and wordy;

- being written using academic language that reads like a Master's thesis or academic article;

- like an academic paper, they take you s-l-o-w-l-y through the details, and the key points are buried right at the end;

- often they get lost in the details and the key points are not apparent at all;

- there is often just one long, detailed phonebook-size evaluation report that some staff member now needs to summarize for top leaders.

[Just think: When this happens, one key group of stakeholders (leaders) never lays eyes directly on the evaluators' work at all! They only get second hand interpretations.]

Characteristics of great evaluation reporting

Great reporting is **succinct**, concise, not unnecessarily wordy, and should never be longer than people will actually read.

Some words of wisdom I received during my industrial and organizational psychology studies were that if you were preparing a report for managers, it should never be longer than a 2-page bullet point summary. For senior managers, it should be a 1-page bullet point summary. For the CEO, it should be a cartoon.

Great reporting is **straightforward**, written in the language and format that works for the readers.

It uses straightforward terms that make sense to non-evaluators. It shouldn't feel like an academic paper or presentation, and it shouldn't be a great effort to read.

Great reporting **gets to the point** — and fast.

You don't feel like you are wading through words looking for what you need to know; what you need to know should be easy to find. The most important points are presented first, which is not only more useful for you; it indicates the evaluation team clearly understands what is most important.

Great reporting **doesn't get lost in the details**; it keeps its eye on the big picture.

The details will be there to support the conclusions, but there is always some synthesis of the information and pulling back to the larger questions.

Great reporting is **layered** with different levels of detail for the different audiences.

There are variations on this, but in general, there should be:

Layer 1: An executive summary of 2 to 3 pages, bullet points or short paragraphs, in straightforward language. This is for an executive audience, so it should be focused on addressing high-level strategic questions.

Layer 2: The main body of the report, about 20 to 30 pages (with plenty of white space, graphs, and pictures) for staff and management. It should answer the evaluation questions and summarize (but not detail) the evidence.

Layer 3: The appendixes are where you should see more detail about the evidence and the methodology, including the all-important steps of how quality and value were defined.

Great evaluation reporting structures

We discussed earlier how actionable evaluation needs evaluative conclusions.

Reporting structures can also help make an evaluation more actionable. Here is one way I have used to structure reports so that they demand actionable answers.

In my experience, the two sections that are by far the most problematic are the Executive Summary and the Findings. What follow are some suggestions for these two sections in particular.

Executive Summary. Specify that the executive summary should be no more than two pages long, have about 7 ± 2 headings, with each heading being one of your key evaluation questions. Under each heading, there should be one to two paragraphs that directly and succinctly answer the question.

Findings. The Findings section should contain 7 ± 2 subheadings, each of which is one of your evaluation questions. The beginning of each section should present a succinct answer to that question — usually the same version found in the executive summary — followed by a summary of the evidence and reasoning that support the conclusion.

Other important elements in a report. Of course, you may require several other sections in the report. One really useful strategy is to consider the sections suggested in Scriven's *Key Evaluation Checklist.*[13]

---

[13] Get the latest KEC at http://michaelscriven.info/

For example, the body of the report should also include items like:

- an <u>Introduction</u>, which explains what the evaluation is, who asked for the evaluation and what its purpose is;

- a <u>Methodology</u> section that explains the methodology used, and *why* that methodology was chosen over other options;

- an explanation of the <u>Context</u> for the evaluation;

- a list of the relevant <u>Values</u> that have been applied in the evaluation, the rationale, and sources; and

- a summary of the <u>Key Evaluation Questions</u>.

~~~~~~~~~~

6. actionable insights

An important aspect of relevant evaluation is actionability. We are looking for answers and insights that are actionable, that people can do something with.

This does <u>not</u> necessarily mean a list of recommendations.

Why giving recommendations may *not* be a good idea

There are three main reasons why specific recommendations for action are generally not a good idea, especially for external evaluators. These are budgetary, political, and psychological.

Budgetary. As an outsider — or even as an insider who was outside senior management – there are often significant budgetary and organizational implications, particularly for major recommendations, that you simply cannot be knowledgeable about. Funding or staff may need to be shifted out of another program or activity, for example. So, there is a danger of suggesting something that is actually completely impractical.

Political. Similarly, there may be issues relating to organizational politics or power structures that would make certain actions unworkable. Again, an outsider could end up making suggestions that simply won't be feasible politically.

Psychological. But the most important issue is actually psychological. If the evaluation team suggests some course of action, psychologically it is perceived as *their* idea, which the organization can choose to adopt or not. As we know from participatory and empowerment approaches, there is something incredibly powerful about being involved in choosing a course of action. It gives people ownership of a decision, a personal stake in it, and a commitment to see it through.

Contrary to popular belief in some circles, recommendations are not a requirement for good, useful, or even actionable evaluation.

As Scriven (1991)[14] aptly put it:

> "Doctors who determine that you are suffering from an incurable disease are not shown to be guilty of misdiagnosis (that is, of having wrongly evaluated your condition) just because they can't come up with a cure. ... A roadtester is not a mechanical engineer, a program evaluator is not a management troubleshooter, though both often suffer from delusions of grandeur in this respect." (pp. 303-304)

---

[14] *Evaluation Thesaurus* http://www.sagepub.com/books/Book3562

Monitoring (what's so) –> evaluative (so what) –> actionable (now what)

Monitoring questions[15] (and their answers) leave the audience to work out whether those findings are any good.

Explicitly evaluative questions ask not just "what's so," but also "so what." They ask which of the findings are really outstanding, which are just adequate, which are weak, and how serious any weaknesses are.

When you have answers to evaluative questions, it's a lot easier to see where action is needed, and how urgent it is. Of course, you do need to ask "what's so" along the way, but the very essence of evaluation is taking the additional step, and also asking "so what" — saying something explicit about quality, value, and importance.

It is worth emphasizing that it is *simply not valid* to go from a value-neutral description of findings to decisions about what actions to take. There is always some need to determine how good the findings are, how serious the weaknesses are, and which are the most important.

In other words, *without the "so what", we can't get to "now what"*.

---

[15] I have previously referred to these as descriptive questions, but as Michael Scriven pointed out in a recent conversation, some descriptions are in fact evaluative. So, I now refer to these as 'monitoring' questions – which seems to me to be a distinction worth making.

What makes evaluation actionable?

So, what are the best options for making evaluation actionable?

First, as I have stressed, make very sure that evaluative questions — the "so what" questions — are asked, and answered explicitly. This is the foundation that is needed to work out what actions to take.

Second, have those with decision-making and budgetary responsibility — and, where appropriate, community members as well — involved in discussing the findings and developing the best course of action. The evaluation team might facilitate this action planning process, or this could be done by someone else who specializes in this kind of work.

For the client organization looking for something more concrete to guide action choices, a useful halfway option is for the evaluation team to suggest two or three broad courses of action, along with the likely trade-offs for each one. This can help clarify the action options, but still allows the client organization, in collaboration with the community, to determine for itself what is going to work best.

~~~~~~~~~~

Conclusions

6.
actionable
insights

1.
clear
purpose

2.
right
engagement

5.
succinct
reporting

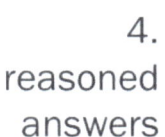

3.
important
questions

4.
reasoned
answers

Let me come back once again to the key elements we need to make sure evaluation is actionable:

1. Crystal clarity about the evaluation's purpose and intended uses — who needs to know what, why, and for what purpose?

2. Engaging the right stakeholders at the right time, particularly in setting the evaluation questions and developing the recommendations and actions.

3. Big-picture evaluation questions to guide the whole evaluation — these should focus on the *quality and value* of what we are doing and achieving (not just 'what' we are doing).

4. A convincing mix of evidence combined with clear evaluative reasoning to give actual answers to the big-picture questions (not just "free associating" to the questions with data).

5. Succinct, straight-to-the-point reporting that doesn't get lost in the details.

6. Answers and insights that are actionable because (a) they are clear about quality, value, and importance and (b) instead of the evaluation team formulating recommendations themselves, there is a sound process (either as part of or following the evaluation) of engaging the right stakeholders in determining the course of action.

If we get these elements right we will have evaluation that is important, useful, influential, and actionable.

Three take-home messages
for actionable evaluation

Finally, let me come back to the three messages I would like you to take away from this book.

Reasoning, not methods. It is incredibly easy to get lost in methods and measurement.

But, as I hope you can see now, evaluation is not just about indicators, metrics, or analysis methods; evaluation is about delivering clear, well-reasoned answers to your most important questions. And it's about using that reasoning to inform smarter decisions about where to concentrate your efforts.

Measurable does not mean important. It is easy to be lured into focusing on things that are easily measured, and on which we can see quick results – but are they really what's most important? Focusing on measurability can prevent us from knowing about – and focusing on – what's really important for sustainable change.

Simple, but not simplistic. Good evaluation presents findings in a way that is simple, but not simplistic. Findings are easy to understand and simply presented; they go right to the heart of what is really important, with no misleading oversimplification.

Great evaluation can provide a succinct, strategic-level snapshot of program performance that captures what's most important. As Michael Scriven says, one of the great skills in evaluation is condensing something from 50 pages to 2 pages *without losing any important information.*

A bonus offer for readers!

All real evaluators understand the importance of reviews to help prospective readers judge whether this book is worth buying for them. Right?

So, please write a review on Amazon.com saying what you found useful or otherwise. In particular, it's really informative to say who would (and would not) benefit from reading this book, and why.

If you do me a favor by posting a review, please email me (Jane@RealEvaluation.com) and let me know, and as a reward, I will send you a FREE copy of an early example of my work!

This is a short piece that blends organizational learning, theory-based evaluation, and evaluative rubrics (this time drawing on a mix of quantitative/survey scales and qualitative/open-ended evidence). It's a PDF of a keynote I did for GIOP, the Gateway Industrial and Organizational Psychologists in July 2002, entitled, *Assessing "Organizational Intelligence": An introduction to the Organizational IQ Test.*

~~~~~~~~~~

Resources & more information

For more information about some of these ideas and concepts, a number of resources are available.

You can find more information about the theory and methodology of evaluative rubrics in my book *Evaluation Methodology Basics: The nuts and bolts of sound evaluation* (2005, Sage Publications): http://realevaluation.com/read/book/

You can also follow the discussion on the Genuine Evaluation blog, which Professor Patricia Rogers and I jointly author: http://GenuineEvaluation.com

If you enjoyed this minibook, you will likely also enjoy my JMDE editorial from 2007 (free PDF): *Unlearning Some of our Social Scientist Habits*. http://journals.sfu.ca/jmde/index.php/jmde_1/article/view/68/71

I'll be putting some more resources on these topics on the blog and my website in the future — **http://RealEvaluation.com** — including guides and tip sheets, online training, and so forth.

Please be sure to sign up for my free newsletter! http://RealEvaluation.com/about/join/

Please also join the conversation by following the Genuine Evaluation blog, following me on:

- twitter **@ejanedavidson**
- **LinkedIn** http://www.linkedin.com/in/realevaluation
- **Facebook** https://www.facebook.com/RealEvaluation

If you have comments or feedback about this book, or suggestions for what you'd like to see next, please email me! jane@RealEvaluation.com

~~~~~~~~~~

About the author

Dr. E. Jane Davidson is internationally recognized for applying critical thinking and evaluative reasoning to evaluation, policy, strategy, and program design. She has a passion for helping organizations ask the most important questions and get straight-to-the-point, actionable answers.

Jane is author of *Evaluation Methodology Basics: The Nuts and Bolts of Sound Evaluation* (Sage Publications, 2005), which has sold well in the U.S. and internationally as a graduate text and evaluation practitioners' guidebook. She brings a distinctively multidisciplinary and refreshingly practical, plain language approach to her work, which spans education, health, social policy, leadership development, and many other areas.

Jane blogs alongside international evaluation expert and author **Professor Patricia J. Rogers** on the entertaining and popular **Genuine Evaluation blog**. Both bloggers share a commitment to improving the quality of evaluation, an unwillingness to accept credentials or power as a substitute for quality, and an international approach from a distinctly Southern Hemisphere perspective.

After completing her doctoral study with Michael Scriven at Claremont Graduate University (California), specializing in organizational psychology with emphasis on evaluation, Jane launched and directed **the world's first fully interdisciplinary Ph.D. in evaluation** (based in the Western Michigan University Evaluation Center). http://www.wmich.edu/evalphd/

Since winning the American Evaluation Association's Marcia Guttentag Award in 2005, Jane has delivered keynote addresses and professional development workshops around the world, in the U.S., the U.K., Brazil, Japan, South Africa, Australia, and New Zealand.

Jane runs a face-to-face and online evaluation consulting and training business, **Real Evaluation Ltd.**, and offers great value-for-money (and some free!) evaluation learning opportunities online.

~~~~~~~~~~

www.ingramcontent.com/pod-product-compliance
Lightning Source LLC
Chambersburg PA
CBHW050818290526
5792CB00001B/162